A TASTE O  D0441515

REAL
Freedom

Beth Moore

LifeWay Press®
Nashville, Tennesee

Published by LifeWay Press®
©Copyright 2009 LifeWay Church Resources

No part of this book may be reproduced or transmitted in any form or by any means, electronic or mechanical, including photocopying and recording, or by any information storage or retrieval system, except as may be expressly permitted in writing by the publisher. Requests for permission should be addressed in writing to LifeWay Press®; One LifeWay Plaza; Nashville, TN 37234-0175.

ISBN 9781415865286 • Item 005139182

Dewey decimal classification: 248.843
Subject Heading: WOMEN-RELIGIOUS LIFE \ BIBLE.O.T. ISAIAH-STUDY AND TEACHING

Scripture quotations identified NIV are from the Holy Bible, New International Version Copyright © 1973, 1978, 1984 by International Bible Society.

To order additional copies of this resource, write LifeWay Church Resources Customer Service; One LifeWay Plaza; Nashville, TN 37234-0113; e-mail *orderentry@lifeway.com;* fax (615) 251-5933; phone toll free (800) 458-2772; order online at *www.lifeway.com;* or visit the LifeWay Christian Store serving you.

Printed in the United States of America

Leadership and Adult Publishing
LifeWay Church Resources
One LifeWay Plaza
Nashville, Tennessee 37234-0175

Contents

Introduction

Scripture asserts that Jesus Christ came forth to "bind up the brokenhearted, to proclaim freedom for the captives and release from darkness for the prisoners … to comfort all who mourn … to bestow on them a crown of beauty for ashes … a garment of praise instead of a spirit of despair" (Isa. 61:1-3).

I had no idea I was one of those "captives" Isaiah mentions until God began to set me free. I received Christ as my Savior when I was a very small child. I never missed a church service or a church-related event. If anyone had told me soon after I surrendered to ministry that Christians could be in bondage, I would have argued with them with all the volume a person can muster with a yoke of slavery strangling her neck. I was the worst kind of captive, a prisoner unaware. The kind of prisoner most vulnerable to her fellow cell mates. Easiest prey there is.

Perhaps you're also unconvinced that Christians can live in bondage. Don't take my word for it. Take God's: "It is for freedom that Christ has set us free. Stand firm, then, and do not let yourselves be burdened again by a yoke of slavery" (Gal. 5:1). Based on Galatians 1:1-2, this liberty plea was directed not at the world but to the church. To genuine believers.

You see, Christ sets us free by the power of His Spirit, then He maintains our freedom as we learn to live from day to day in the power of His free Spirit. It is how to hold onto that daily freedom that we are addressing. How do we overcome the obstacles that bind us to feelings of defeat and despair?

Beloved, God wants to do in your life what your eyes have never seen, your ears have never heard, and your mind has never conceived. But just as the children of Israel were held captive by the Babylonians, areas of captivity can keep us from living out the abundant life God has for us.

As we begin, understand that a Christian is held captive by anything that hinders the full and effective Spirit-filled life God planned for her.

When I realized God was calling me to write this study, I asked the group of women I teach to broaden my horizon in terms of areas of captivity believers can face. I asked any of them who had been set free from an area of bondage to consider sharing two things with me through a letter:

- the specific area of captivity they faced, and
- the specific ways and lengths of time God employed to set them free.

I'm not sure that anything could have prepared me for their responses. These women are bright, educated Christians. They serve faithfully in their churches. Many sing in the choir. They come from all economic backgrounds. For fear of judgment many of them have never told anyone but a godly counselor what they battled.

I heard painful testimonies of bondage to lust and a pattern of falling into sexual sin. I tearfully read about struggles with homosexuality and fear of men because of childhood abuse. Some spoke about a previous inability to love people fully, including their own husbands and children. One wrote me about the victory she'd found over the compulsion to steal. Another had been freed from habitual dishonesty. A friend I never would have suspected wrote me about her freedom from the bitterness flowing from the physical abuse she endured as a child. My heart broke for one woman who described how deep insecurity had stolen friends, church work, and a contented marriage from her. I've heard from many who were held captive by a critical and judgmental heart toward people. Others had wrestled terribly with anger toward God. Doubt. Discouragement. Loneliness. A chronic lack of satisfaction.

Remember, these letters were only from those who had found freedom in Christ. Imagine how many are still struggling! Believer,

- Christ came to set the captives free—no matter what kind of yokes bind them.
- Christ came to bind up the brokenhearted—no matter what broke their hearts.
- He came to open the eyes of the blind—no matter what veiled their vision.

Throughout the next pages, I want to introduce you to the idea that one of the most effective ways we can detect an area of captivity is to measure whether or not we are enjoying the benefits God intends for every child of God.

According to the Book of Isaiah, God has graciously extended the following benefits to His children.

To know God and believe Him. *Isaiah 43:10*

To glorify God. *Isaiah 43:7*

To find satisfaction in God. *Isaiah 55:2*

To experience God's peace. *Isaiah 48:12*

To enjoy God's presence. *Isaiah 43:2-3*

My dear friend, these five benefits will serve as a road map to lead you home when you've been carried away captive by any form of bondage. In these next few pages, we'll take a closer look at each benefit and will identify the obstacles that keep us from embracing the freedom God offers.

*With Christ's help,
we can live each day
in liberty.*

Believe
Overcome
Your Unbelief

"You are my witnesses,"

declares the L<small>ORD</small>,

   "and my servant whom

    I have chosen,

so that you may know and believe me

   and understand that I am he.

Before me no god was formed,

   nor will there be one after me.

I, even I, am the L<small>ORD</small>,

   and apart from me there is no savior.

I have revealed and saved

and proclaimed—

   I, and not some foreign

   god among you.

You are my witnesses," declares

the L<small>ORD</small>, "that I am God."

Isaiah 43:10–12

Beloved, Scripture makes clear that we have been chosen to "know" and "believe" God. But in order to truly embrace these truths, we need to better understand what they really mean. Let's begin in Isaiah 43:10 where the Hebrew word for know is *yadha.* This ancient term encompasses a very personal level of familiarity and was often used to depict a close relationship between a husband and wife. One of your chief purposes on this planet is to know God intimately and with reverent familiarity.

John 8:36 tells us how this intimate relationship is to begin. It says, "If the Son sets you free, you will be free indeed." Only by accepting the reality that God allowed His Son, Jesus, to be sacrificed on the cross for our sins and agreeing with Him that we are sinners in need of salvation are we able to approach God with confidence.

Only through a relationship with Jesus Christ are we in a position to "know" God. Before we proceed, ask yourself, "Have I really accepted Jesus Christ as my personal

Savior?" If your answer is "no" or even "I'm not certain," I cannot think of a better time than right now to do so.

One of the most beautiful elements of salvation is its simplicity. Christ has already done all the work on the cross. All you must do is …

1. Acknowledge you are a sinner and cannot save yourself.
2. Acknowledge that Christ is the Son of God and only He can save you.
3. Believe His crucifixion was for your personal sins, and His death was in your behalf.
4. Give Him your life and ask Him to be your Savior and Lord.

Yes, it really is that easy!

If you are already enjoying a close relationship with God, these next pages will provide an opportunity to deepen your relationship. If you can't characterize your relationship with God with words like *close* and *familiar*, don't despair! As we allow God to penetrate our hearts, mend them, change them, or simply make them more like His own, we will have priceless opportunities to get in tune with His heart and know Him.

Isaiah 43:10 tells us that God not only desires for us to know Him but He also wants us to believe Him! The Hebrew word for believe in this verse means "to trust."

The level of trust we have for God is a monumental issue in the life of every believer. Many variables in our lives affect our willingness to trust God. A painful loss or a dreadful betrayal can deeply mark our level of trust. A broken heart never mended by the one true Healer handicaps us terribly when we're challenged to trust. Trusting an invisible God is not something that comes naturally to any believer. A trust relationship grows only one way: by stepping out in faith and making the choice to trust. This step can sometimes seem more than we can take, but God is anxious to help us overcome.

It's important to recognize the ability to believe God develops most often through pure experience. "I found Him faithful yesterday. He will not be unfaithful today."

If we feel hindered in our process of knowing God and believing Him, something is holding us back. As simplistic as it seems, the largest obstacle we have in believing God is unbelief, choosing not to believe Him. Today I'm not talking about believing in God. I'm talking about believing God, believing what He says, and believing He is Who He says He is.

Let's get at the phrase "believing God" to have a better understanding of its greatly hindering antonym. Genesis 15:6 says, "Abram believed the LORD, and he credited it to him as righteousness." In Genesis 15:6, the Hebrew word for believed is 'Aman meaning "to make firm, … to stand firm, to be enduring; to trust, to believe." In the Old Testament, the Hebrew word is often translated into the English word faithful.

In Romans 4:3 Abraham's belief in God is once again credited to him as "righteousness." Here, the Greek word for believed is *pisteuo* meaning "to be firmly persuaded as to something, to believe … with the idea of hope and certain expectation." It comes from the Greek word *pistis,* translated into the English word faith throughout the New Testament. Throughout the Bible, belief and faith represent the same concept.

Now let's take a closer look at the concept of unbelief. In Mark 9:21-24, as the desperate father of a demon-possessed child stood in the presence of Christ, he could no longer hold back his honest heart: "Help me overcome my unbelief!" Though he sought Christ's healing and freedom for his son, the man struggled to put total faith in Him. The Greek word for unbelief is *apistos,* meaning "not worthy of confidence, untrustworthy … a thing not to be believed, incredible." As we view this definition along with those of belief and faith, we can safely draw the following conclusion: We can believe in Christ, accepting the truth that He is the Son of God, and we can believe on Christ, receiving eternal salvation, yet fail to stand firm, endure in belief and choose to find Him trustworthy day to day. The phrase "not worthy of confidence" almost makes me shudder. God is so deserving of our trust. How can we not believe Him?

Beloved, unbelief is crippling. Second Corinthians 5:7 says, "For we walk by faith, not by sight" (KJV). In other words, the steps we take forward with God we take through faith or belief. Therefore, unbelief literally cripples our spiritual walk, casting huge obstacles in the way of a victorious journey here on earth.

We sometimes approach Christ with the attitude of the father with the demon-possessed boy. But we must get our hearts and minds around the idea that God always wills the spiritual captive to be free. God's will is for us to know Him and believe Him, glorify Him, be satisfied in Him, experience peace in Him, and enjoy Him. For God to have utmost cooperation from us on this freedom trail, we must believe that He is willing and that He is completely able.

Perhaps you secretly approach God with the attitude, "if you can do anything, take pity on me." But if we're willing to admit our lack of confidence in Him rather than allowing doubt to overshadow our faith, Christ is more than willing to help us overcome our unbelief. Belief (or faith in the abilities and promises of God) is a vital prerequisite for fleshing out the liberty we've won through Christ Jesus.

The most effective key to believing God is right before our eyes: the more we know Him, the more we will believe Him. The apostle Paul said it best: "I know whom I have believed, and am convinced that he is able to guard what I have entrusted to him for that day" (2 Tim. 1:12).

We tend to run to God for temporary relief. God is looking for people who will walk with Him in steadfast belief. Beloved, choose to believe. Choose to know the One who is completely worthy of our trust.

Glorify God

Take Yourself Off the Throne

They were calling to one another:

"Holy, holy, holy is the

LORD Almighty;

the whole earth is full of his glory."

Isaiah 6:3

Moses and Aaron went from the assembly to the entrance to the Tent of Meeting and fell facedown, and the glory of the LORD appeared to them.

Numbers 20:6

Ever wonder why God created us? According to Isaiah 43:7, we are created for His glory. But what does that really mean? The more I study the concept of God's glory, the more convinced I become that it is almost indefinable. Keep in mind, however, that God's glory far exceeds anything we can humanly comprehend. His glory is everything we're about to learn and infinitely more.

Let's begin with a look at how Scripture presents the concept of God's glory:

As these passages suggest, God's glory is something that reflects Him. But more mysteriously, it is also part of who He is! In each of those Old Testament references, the Hebrew word for glory is *kavodh* meaning "weight, honor, esteem." The word *kavodh* comes from another Hebrew term that greatly increases our comprehension. The word *kavedh* means to "be renowned … to show oneself great or mighty." In other words, glory is the way God makes Himself known or shows Himself mighty. The Lord wants to reveal Himself to humans. Each way He accomplishes this divine task is His glory. God's glory is how He shows who He is.

The Greek word often used for glory in New Testament references is *doxa*. It is "the true apprehension of God or things. The glory of God must mean His unchanging essence. Giving glory to God is ascribing to Him His full recognition ... The glory of God is what He is essentially." God's glory is the way He makes Himself recognizable.

I believe being created for God's glory means two marvelous truths to those who are called by His name. In short, God wants to make Himself recognizable *to* and *through* us.

Living a life that glorifies God is synonymous with living a life that reveals God. We glorify God to the degree that we externalize the internal existence of the living Christ. We were created for the purpose of giving His invisible character a glimpse of visibility. In other words, we fulfill what we were "meant to be" when God is "recognizable" in our lifestyle.

If you're like me, you're probably overwhelmed by the enormous responsibility of such a calling. We're imperfect creatures! How are we to help others recognize something about God just from watching our lives and knowing us? Consider another portion of the definition of *doxa* that relates the term to humans: "the glory of created things including man is what they are meant by God to be, though not yet perfectly attained."

Not yet perfectly attained ... Many of us learned Romans 3:23 in Sunday School. God intended that we show forth His glory, but we have "all have sinned and fall short of the glory of God" (Rom. 3:23). We've fallen short, missed the mark, sinned; but anyone who knows our God knows He is far too tenacious to be thwarted by our sin. Paul declares that "God has chosen to make known among the Gentiles the glorious riches of this mystery, which is Christ in you, the hope of glory" (Col. 1:27). The apostle Paul announced the mystery that Christ Himself dwells in the life of every believer. Christ in us! Romans 8:9

tells us that "if anyone does not have the Spirit of Christ, he does not belong to Christ." In other words, the moment each of us received Christ as our Savior, the Holy Spirit of Christ took up residence in our inner being.

Do you see the key? We have no hope whatsoever of God being recognizable in us if the Spirit of Christ does not dwell in us. If we are not occupied by the Holy Spirit, we have nothing of God in us for Him to show. Christ is a human's only "hope of glory"!

Remember, God is glorified in anyone through whom He is allowed to show Himself ... and show Himself great or mighty. But to fulfill our God-given destinies—to allow the King of all creation to show Himself through us—we must overcome the temptation to seek our own glory by desiring His instead. If we are to recognize and allow God to free us from any areas of captivity, we must recognize a major obstace in living up to the purpose for which we were created. That obstace is pride.

Pride is more than self-promotion. It is a dangerous lure to captivity. Why?

- God wants to get to our hearts. Pride covers the heart.
- God wants to free us from any hindrances in our past. Pride refuses to take a fresh look back.
- God wants to treat us with the prescription of His Word. Pride doesn't like to be told what to do.
- God wants to set us completely free. Pride thinks he's free enough.
- God wants to bring us out of dark closets. Pride says secrets are nobody else's business.
- God wants to help us with problems. Pride denies there is a problem.
- God wants to make us strong in Him. Pride won't admit to weakness.

Beloved, pride is a vicious enemy. God hates pride because it involves dethroning Him and putting ourselves at the center of our universe. I believe God's hatred of pride expresses

His love. Pride slights Him but destroys us. We must learn to view humility as a friend. Only when we humble ourselves before God, acknowledging that He is great and we are not, do we prepare our hearts to glorify God.

A simple reality check should make humbling ourselves achievable. Just read a few Scriptures boasting in the greatness of God; Job 38 is one of my favorites. We don't have to look hard to see how small we are in comparison to God and to respond appropriately by bowing down before Him. In a nutshell, that's what humbling ourselves before God means: that we bow down before His majesty.

Second Corinthians 3:17-18 says we are being changed into Christ's "likeness with ever-increasing glory." You see, people who are living out the reality of their liberation in Christ progress in their spiritual lives in an "ever-increasing glory." As they grow in spiritual maturity, the Spirit of Christ becomes easily recognizable in them. A life that glorifies God or makes Him recognizable is a process that ideally progresses with time and maturity. It is evidenced when...

- our most important consideration in every undertaking is whether or not God could be glorified (1 Cor. 10:31).
- we do not seek our own glory (John 8:50, 54).
- our sincere hope in our service to others is that they will somehow see God through us (1 Pet. 4:10-11).
- we go through hardships and turn to God and try to cooperate with Him so He can use them for our good and for His glory (1 Pet. 4:12-13).
- we recognize we are sometimes able to accomplish or withstand things only through the power of God (2 Cor. 4:7).

No matter where you are on this journey to the glorifying, liberated life in Christ, you are His treasure. You may feel like you have a long way to go before you are fulfilling His purpose. Instead, I hope you can see the magnificent potential He planned for you to fulfill. On the other hand, you may be able to celebrate some progress in your pursuit of a God-glorifying life. No matter what God has exposed to you, relish the wonderful words of Christ that pertain to you. From the shadow of the cross, He said of you:

> I pray for them. I am not praying for the world, but for those you have given me, for they are yours. All I have is yours, and all you have is mine. And glory has come to me through them.
>
> *John 17:9-10*

That's right, my friend, glory comes to Jesus through you!

Find Satisfaction in God

Overcome Idolatry

Things started changing, and healing began

Why spend money on what is not bread,
and your labor on what does not
satisfy?
Listen, listen to me, and eat what is good,
and your soul will delight in the
richest of fare.

Isaiah 55:2

In Isaiah 55:2 God posed the question that haunts every generation of Adam's descendants. "Why spend money on what is not bread, and your labor on what does not satisfy?" Then, like a frustrated parent determined to get through to his child, He said, "Listen, listen to me, and eat what is good, and your soul will delight in the richest of fare." Many of us seek satisfaction in the next promotion, a bigger house, another baby, or a new hairstyle, but these fixes do little to get at the underlying disease of discontent that plagues us.

This passage is not as much about financial decisions and work as it is about an important spiritual concept, finding contentment in the Lord rather than in the world. I believe God's prescription for those who possess an inner thirst (Isa. 55:1) and hunger they cannot fill is implied in Isaiah 55:6: Those who are spiritually thirsty and hungry need to "Seek the Lord."

I also believe God creates a nagging dissatisfaction in everyone for an excellent reason. According to 2 Peter 3:9, God doesn't want anyone to perish. Rather, He wants everyone to come to repentance. He gave us a will so we could choose whether to accept His invitation: "come to me." God purposely created us with a need only He can meet, a spiritual "hunger" that only He can satisfy.

The filling God alone can give does not automatically accompany our salvation. I was in my early 30's before I understood the huge difference between salvation from sin and satisfaction of soul. Salvation secures our lives for all eternity. Soul satisfaction insures abundant life on earth.

We can learn several truths about satisfied souls by drawing a parallel between the soul and the physical body. I know this seems simplistic, but humor me. How do you know you are hungry? when you are thirsty?

Continue to humor me here. What do you usually do when you're hungry or thirsty? You seek what will meet your need. If you ignore your physical needs long enough, not only will you be miserable, you will be ill.

You can easily recognize the signals the body gives, but great wisdom lies in learning to discern the signals your spiritual nature gives. Psalm 63 offers insight into the satisfied soul. Look at David's descriptions of satisfaction: "my soul thirsts for you, my body longs for you, in a dry and weary land" (v. 1). "Because your love is better than life, my lips will glorify you" (v. 3). "My soul will be satisfied as with the richest of foods (v. 5). The most obvious symptom of a soul in need of God's satisfaction is a sense of inner emptiness. The awareness of a "hollow place" somewhere deep inside—the inability to be satisfied.

Our infinitely wise and merciful Lord makes every one of us with a God-shaped void in our lives so we will seek Him. Dissatisfaction is not a terrible thing. It's a God-thing. Only Jesus is absolutely satisfying. In fact, He is the only means by which any mortal creature can find true satisfaction.

Many come to Christ out of their search for something missing; yet after receiving His salvation, they go elsewhere for further satisfaction. Christians can be miserably dissatisfied if they accept Christ's salvation yet reject the fullness of daily relationship that satisfies like a warm, well-rounded meal on an empty stomach. You may ask, "Can't I find similar contentment through spending time with my kids? through charity work and service to my church?" The answer, Beloved, is no. Though important, these are just activities. The only answer to our soul dissatisfaction is deep relationship with God.

God gave the practice of settling for satisfaction in things other than Him a name I was unprepared to hear: idolatry. After serious meditation, I realized the label made perfect sense no matter how harsh it seemed. Anything we try to put in a place where God belongs is an idol.

Can you see the strong tie between our quest for satisfaction and the worship of idols? The void God created in our lives for Himself will demand attention. We look desperately for something to satisfy us and fill the empty places. Our craving to be filled is so strong that the moment something or someone seems to meet our need, we feel an overwhelming temptation to worship it.

Some of the idols in our lives—things or people we have put in God's place—have been in those places for years, and only the power of God can make them budge. We must begin to remove idols by choosing to recognize their existence and admitting their inability to keep us satisfied.

Beloved, whatever we are gripping to bring us the satisfaction is a lie—unless it is Christ. He is the Truth that sets us free. If you are holding anything in your craving for satisfaction right now, would you be willing to acknowledge it as a lie? Even if you feel you can't let go of it right this moment, would you lift it before Him—perhaps literally lifting your fisted hand as a symbol—and confess it as an idol? God does not condemn you. He calls you. Will you open your hand to Him?

Take heart. Each of us has succumbed to idolatry at times in our lives. Before you hang your head in shame, remember that the Holy Spirit does not convict us of sin to condemn us. Rather, He convicts us of sin so we'll become fully aware, seek forgiveness, and be set free!

The mercy of God is indescribable, isn't it? Even when His people, the Israelites, repeatedly turned to idols, He swept away their offenses like a cloud, their sins like the morning mist. As we face some of the idols we have worshiped in our quest for satisfaction, we need never doubt the mercy of God. He asks one thing: "'Return to me, for I have redeemed you'" (Isa. 44: 22).

A very crucial part of fleshing out our liberation in Christ means allowing Him to fill the empty places in our lives. Satisfaction in Christ can be a reality. I know from experience, and I want everyone to know how complete He can make us feel. I'm not talking about a life full of activities. I'm talking about a soul full of Jesus.

Chapter 4

Experience God's Peace

Overcome Prayerlessness

Now may the Lord of peace himself give you peace at all times and in every way. The Lord be with all of you.

2 Thessalonians 3:16

Life is busy. For many of us, just getting through the daily routine means managing controlled chaos. I don't believe I can over-emphasize the importance of peace as a real and practical benefit of our covenant relation-ship with God. His peace should not be an infrequent surprise but the ongoing rule of our lives. Peace can be possible in any situation, but we cannot simply produce it on demand. In fact, we cannot produce it at all. It is "fruit of the Spirit" (Gal. 5:22).

Each believer has Christ's peace. It was given to us when we accepted salvation. We just don't always know how to activate it.

I believe Christ grieves when He sees our hearts in unnecessary turmoil. He desires that we find rest in Him. You can have the peace of Christ, believer, no matter what your circumstances; but you must learn how to receive it.

In Isaiah 48:18, the peace God offers is compared to a river. Consider the following applications as you get your mind around this important analogy.

A river is a moving stream of water. God's Word does not say we'll have peace like a pond. If we were honest, we might admit to thinking of peaceful people as boring. We may think, "I'd rather forego peace and have an exciting life!" Beloved, few bodies of water are more exciting than rivers! When was the last time you saw white-water rapids? We can have active, exciting lives without suffering through a life of turmoil.

When God used the analogy of a river, He described a peace that can be retained while life twists and turns and rolls over boulders. To have peace like a river is to have security and tranquillity while meeting many bumps and unexpected turns on life's journey.

So how can we tap into this peace God offers? The answer is in what not to do.

For many of us, our typical approach to life's stresses reads like this: "Do not be calm about anything, but in everything, by dwelling on it constantly and feeling picked on by God, with thoughts like 'and this is the thanks I get,' present your aggravations to everyone you know but Him. And the acid in your stomach, which transcends all milk products, will cause you an ulcer, and the doctor bills will cause you a heart attack and you will lose your mind."

Without a doubt, avoiding prayer is a sure prescription for anxiety, a certain way to avoid peace. Peace comes from an active, ongoing, and obedient relationship with the Prince of Peace. He wants to feed us with the Living Water of His Holy Spirit and a steady stream of His Word until we have peace like a river.

The path to peace is paved with knee-prints. The enemy knows the power of prayer. He's been watching it furiously for thousands of years.

I searched for all the uses of the word pray in its various forms from Genesis to Revelation. I nearly wept as I saw hundreds of references.

Abraham prayed … Isaac prayed …
Jacob prayed … Moses left Pharaoh
and prayed … So Moses prayed for the
people … Manoah prayed to the Lord …
Samson prayed … Hannah wept much
and prayed … So David prayed … Elijah
stepped forward and prayed … And
Elisha prayed, "O, Lord" … After Job had
prayed for his friends … And Hezekiah
prayed to the Lord … Daniel got down
on his knees and prayed … From inside
the fish Jonah prayed … Very early in
the morning, while it was still dark, Jesus
got up, left the house and went off to a
solitary place, where He prayed …
Going a little farther, He fell with his
face to the ground and prayed.

Christ sought to have the divine life strengthened in Him through times of intimacy with the Father. How much more should I? I'm hopeless to live victoriously without prayer.

The Bible is a Book of Prayer. And God's presence is a house of prayer (Isa. 56:7). O, Beloved, when the record of our days stands complete, may the words have been written of us, "Then he or she prayed …"

Peace is the fruit of an obedient, righteous life. To experience the kind of peace that covers all circumstances, the Bible challenges us to develop active, authentic (what I call "meaty") prayer lives. Prayer with real substance—original thoughts flowing from a highly individual heart, personal and intimate. Often, we do everything *but* pray. Even studying the Bible, going to church, talking to the pastor, or receiving counsel seems more tangible than prayer.

But the better we know God (Eph. 1:17), the more we will trust Him. The more we trust Him, the more we will sense His peace. Prayer matters. God's Spirit released through our prayers and the prayers of others turns cowards into conquerors, chaos into calm, cries into comfort. By staying in constant communication with God, we receive a continual supply of strength to walk victoriously in peace even as we walk through a war zone.

This world doesn't have lasting solutions to life's stresses and strains. Its best advice seems to be: just remember two things—*don't sweat the small stuff* and *it's all small stuff.* Just once I'd like to stuff a sock into the mouth of the person who first said that because it's *not* all small stuff. My friend's son was paralyzed in an accident his senior year. I pray almost daily for a list of people who are battling cancer. Two recently came off my list and into heaven. An honest, hardworking believer just lost his job—again. Not long ago, tornadoes whipped through my hometown—stealing, killing, and destroying. No, it's not all small stuff. Worldly philosophy minimizes difficulty because it has no real answers, but we know better than to buy the small-stuff philosophy.

Remember, peace comes in situations completely surrendered to Christ's sovereign authority. Sometimes when we stop looking for all the answers to the "why's" in our lives and decide to trust a sovereign God, unexpected peace washes over us. We must remember that bending the knee is ultimately a matter of pure obedience. You may never feel like giving your circumstance, hurt, or loss to Him; but you can choose to submit to His authority out of belief and obedience rather than emotion. Obedience is always the mark of authentic surrender to God's authority.

The key to peace is, "He will be called … Prince of Peace. Of the increase of his government and peace there will be no end" (Isa. 9:6-7). Beloved, let God write this on your heart forever: The key to peace is authority. When we allow the Prince of Peace, Jesus Christ, to govern our lives, peace either immediately or ultimately results.

Beloved, peace is not beyond reach. If you have not yet bowed the knee to God's authority over your past, something is holding you captive. If you grant God complete access to your heart, mind, and soul, you will be free to rest in Him.

Take pleasure in knowing that God inspired His Word with great care and immaculate precision. He chose every word purposely. When He said we could have peace like a river (Isa. 48:18), He meant it. What does it take? Paying close attention to God's commands (by obedience) through the power of the Holy Spirit within us. Why should we? Because God is incapable of making mistakes. He teaches us only what is best for us (Isa. 48:17) and directs us only in the way we should go. Obedience to God's authority not only brings peace like a river but righteousness like the waves of the sea. Not righteous perfection. Righteous consistency.

Bow to His trustworthy authority. Surrender every part of your life and every concern of your heart to the all-powerful, all-sufficent, all-knowing Creator. In short, "Let the peace of Christ rule in your hearts" (Col. 3:15).

Enjoy God's Presence

Beware of Legalism

When you pass through the waters,

    I will be with you;

and when you pass through the rivers,

    they will not sweep over you.

When you walk through the fire,

    you will not be burned;

    the flames will not set you ablaze.

For I am the LORD, your God,

    the Holy One of Israel.

Isaiah 43:2-3

When was the last time you felt the warm, comforting glow of God's presence enveloping you? the confident assurance that He's alongside you, holding your hand when life gets rough? I doubt any believer feels God's wonderful presence every second of every day. After all, frightening things can happen to believers as well as unbelievers, and difficult things happen to His children, too. Sometimes we're challenged to simply believe He's with us because He's promised (Heb. 13:5). And that assurance of His abiding presence should calm all our fears. But while Scripture repeatedly assures believers that God is with us and that God's presence in our lives is absolutely unchanging, the evidence of His presence is not.

I believe that on some occasions God may purposely alter the evidences of His presence in order to bring the most benefit from our experience. Sometimes we receive the most benefit from seeing many visible "prints" of His invisible hands during a difficult season. Other times, we profit most from seeing fewer evidences. God does not love us less when He gives us fewer evidences. He simply desires to grow us up and teach us to walk by faith.

In Matthew 14:25-32 in the midst of a storm Jesus came walking on the water. To His terrified disciples, He said: "Take courage! It is I. Don't be afraid," but the storm continued to rage until He got into the boat. The point is not that we have nothing to fear but that His presence is the basis for our courage. Christ did not say, "Take courage! I am calming the storm. Don't be afraid." Instead, with the winds still raging, He said, "Take courage! It is I. Don't be afraid."

Christ does not always immediately calm the storms in our lives, but He is always willing to calm His child on the basis of His presence. "Don't worry! I know the winds are raging and the waves are high, but I am God over both. If I let them continue to swell, it's because I want you to see Me walk on the water." We'll probably never learn to enjoy our storms, but we can learn to enjoy God's presence in the storm!

In Psalm 16:11, King David confidently proclaimed that God would "fill" him with "joy in [His] presence." The New King James Version says, "In Your presence there is fullness of joy!" The Hebrew word for joy means, "glee, gladness, joy, pleasure, rejoice(-ing.)" We can learn to enjoy God's presence even when life is not presently enjoyable. I can't explain it, but I've experienced it personally over and over.

No relationship in my life brings me more joy than my relationship with God. I certainly haven't "arrived" in some mystical place, nor have I made even these few steps quickly or casually. I've grown to enjoy God with time. Not every minute I spend with Him is gleeful or great fun. Intimacy with God grows through sharing every realm of experience. I've wept bitterly with Him. I've screamed in frustration. Sometimes I thought He was going to break my heart in two. But I've also laughed out loud with Him. Wept with unspeakable joy. Left the chair and gone to my knees in awe. Squealed with excitement.

I've been to every extremity and back with God. But if I had to define my relationship with Him by one general statement, I would tell you He is the absolute joy of my life. I don't just love Him. I love loving Him.

My friend, I want God to be the greatest reality in your life. I want you to be more assured of His presence than any other you can see or touch. This can be your reality. This is your right as a child of God. We were destined for this kind of relationship with God, but the enemy tries to convince us that the Christian life is sacrificial at best and artificial at worst.

Many elements or conditions can keep us from truly enjoying God's presence in our personal lives. For instance, not spending adequate time with Him would affect our pure enjoyment of His presence. Having an underdeveloped prayer life could also rob our joy as could harboring bitterness or anger at another person. But the person who studies God's Word in depth and still experiences a consistent lack of enjoyment of God often suffers from a condition with an ugly name: legalism.

Isaiah 29:13 explains it best: "The Lord says: 'These people come near to me with their mouth and honor me with their lips, but their hearts are far from me. Their worship of me is made up only of rules taught by men.' "

I am so thankful to testify that I have seen far more genuine examples of true Christianity in the church than unfeeling legalists. Unfortunately, I have also seen many caring Christians intimidated by the occasional legalist. Concentrating on the shortcomings of others can cheat a Christian of truly enjoying the presence of God.

In my opinion, legalism results when three conditions occur:

1. Regulations replace relationship. The Pharisees in Matthew 12 had a superficial understanding of God and no enjoyment of His presence. The Sabbath belonged entirely to God. He established it for man's benefit, not his imprisonment. The greatest benefit Christ could bring to the man with the shriveled hand was a relationship with the Savior. He initiated that relationship through healing, disregarding the old regulations that might label the healing as "work" and therefore an unacceptable Sabbath activity. As students of God's Word, we need to be mindful of keeping the enjoyment in our Christian walk and not replacing it with regulations.

2. Microscopes replace mirrors. Modern-day Pharisees sometimes practice religious voyeurism, looking for a reason to accuse others. They tend to love a church "soap opera" because their own relationship with God is so unexciting. They look to the faults of others to keep things interesting. They stop examining the conditions of their own hearts before the Father, instead looking intently for the shortcomings in their fellow believers. Sadly, this is often in an attempt to mentally claim, "Well, at least I don't do as so-and-so."

3. Performance replaces passion. If our motivation for obedience is anything other than love and devotion for God, we're probably up to our eyeballs in legalism and in for disaster. God isn't concerned whether our voices can carry a tune or they take the lead in an opera. His concern is the passion behind the singing. Behind any effort meant for Him. Hearts full of zeal for God far outweigh activities designed to please Him. Obedience without love is nothing but the law. To expereince God's presence, we must passionately desire Him more than anything else.

Beloved, God does not take our spiritual temperature under the tongue by the words we say, nor in our ear by the impressive teachings we hear, nor under our arms by the service we perform. God takes our spiritual temperature straight from the heart.

That's why it's so important that we recognize the following about our journey with the Lord:

1. This journey is about a relationship—not regulations. I want you to thoroughly enjoy God's presence. I am praying for you to sense His presence more than ever. If you ask Him to make Himself real to you through His Word and lavish you with His love, you will enjoy God even when you don't enjoy the confrontation. God is going to get very personal with us if we take breaking free seriously. Sometimes you're going to have your eyes opened to things you'd rather not see. How do I know? Because I've been on this journey!

2. This journey is about you. In the past, I've written about biblical figures like Moses, David, and Paul. This time each of us is the human protagonist, and we can let God's Word become a mirror of what we want reflected in our lives.

3. This journey is about the heart. Bible study is for the heart—to loosen any chains withholding the heart from enjoying the abundant liberty in Christ's salvation. I plead with you to withhold nothing from God as you journey toward freedom in Christ.

Precious student of God's Word, God's specialty is rolling away a stone. Show Him which obstacle to freedom in Him is causing you trouble, put your hands on top of His, and on the count of three …

Conclusion

You and I must want nothing less than God's best. Throughout this booklet, we have exerted spiritual muscle in rolling away the stones of …

Unbelief …
  so we may know God and believe Him.
Pride …
  so we may glorify God.
Idolatry…
  so we may find satisfaction in God.
Prayerlessness …
  so we can experience God's peace.

Dear friend, the enemy has no right to hold you back from any of these benefits. They are yours. Realize that Christ gave up everything so you could be free. The cross purchased your freedom from every yoke and replaced it with one to Christ Himself (Matt. 11:28-30). Nothing can hold you captive without your permission. Don't go back to slavery! Jesus did not set you free for you to live the rest of your life in self-inflicted bondage! Learn to live in Christ's glorious liberty; then stay on the alert so you don't return to captivity!

Beloved, if our liberty in Christ is going to be a reality in life, we are going to have to learn to walk in the freedom of Christ, independent of everyone else we know. In our quest for freedom, we don't just need a leader. Someone could lead us to freedom, and we could still return to captivity.

We need more than a leader on our road to freedom. We need someone to stick around and empower us to remain free. We need a Savior who keeps on saving. Many people think of salvation as their initial invitation for Christ to forgive them and come into their lives. Although we need to be saved from eternal separation from God only once,

Christ continues His saving work in us for the rest of our lives.

Commit yourself entirely to God that He may set you free to be everything He planned. Ask Him in Jesus' name not to let the enemy steal one bit of the victory God has for you. We must not allow intimidation or fear to imprison us in any area. Remember, Satan can presume no authority in your life. He will do his best to bluff you. Don't let him. "The one who is in you is greater than the one who is in the world" (1 John 4:4).

Listen closely.
The liberty bell's ringing.

BETH MOORE

ASK A QUESTION,
GRAB A FRIEND,
START A STUDY,
CHANGE YOUR LIFE.

How do I ...
fight the good fight?

Do you ever feel inadequate, threatened, or pushed into situations that seem

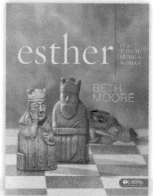

overpowering? The Old Testament story of Esther provides a faithful example of courage for today's woman. Her destiny can be yours as you get to know more deeply the God who is in your corner with ***Esther: It's Tough Being a Woman***.

LIFEWAY.COM/WOMEN | 1.800.458.2772

LifeWay | Women